D0191629

Take a look inside my home

Rainforest

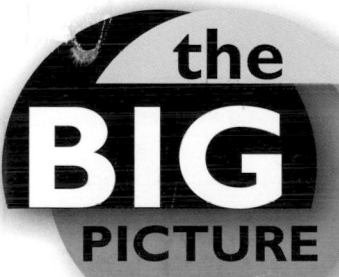
the **BIG** PICTURE

Sarah Levete

Published 2010 by
A&C Black Publishers Ltd.
36 Soho Square, London, W1D 3QY

www.acblack.com

ISBN HB 978-1-4081-2786-5
         PB 978-1-4081-3153-4

This book is produced using paper that is made from wood grown in managed, sustainable forests. It is natural, renewable and recyclable. The logging and manufacturing processes conform to the environmental regulations of the country of origin.

Produced for A&C Black by Calcium. www.calciumcreative.co.uk

Printed and bound in China by C&C Offset Printing Co.

All the internet addresses given in this book were correct at the time of going to press. The author and publishers regret any inconvenience caused if addresses have changed or sites have ceased to exist, but can accept no responsibility for any such changes.

Acknowledgements

The publishers would like to thank the following for their kind permission to reproduce their photographs:

Cover: Shutterstock: Tom C Amon (front), Ethylalkohol (back). **Pages:** Fotolia: Roman Shiyanov 19; Shutterstock: Galyna Andrushko 6-7, Anyka 6-7, Matthew Cole 16, Ethylalkohol 14, Frontpage 20-21, Eric Gevaert 1, 8, Eric Isselée 11, Kkaplin 9, 24, Timur Kulgarin 13, Michael Lynch 17, Steve Mann 8-9, Antonio Jorge Nunes 4-5, 16-17, Dr. Morley Read 2-3, 15, 18-19, 22-23, Rsfatt 3, Chai Kian Shin 5, Szefei 14-15, Charles Taylor 20-21, Wouter Tolenaars 10-11, Tonobalaguerf 12-13, Worldswildlifewonders 10.

Contents

Rainforest

This green, leafy place is bursting with tall trees, plants, and animals.

Sunshine and rain

Rainforests grow in places where there is a lot of rain and sunshine.

Hot and wet

Gobble gobble

Some plants eat animals in rainforests. The **pitcher plant** traps animals and insects. Then it eats them!

A pitcher plant can grow as tall as a house.

Lots of Rain

It is hot in the rainforest.
It rains most of the time,
but it is sunny too.

No sun below

Rainforest trees are very tall.
Their huge leaves catch
the sun so it is dark
on the ground.

*Many rainforest
animals like
the rain.*

Raining again

Raindrops fall onto rainforest leaves. They dry in the sun, then rise back into the air. Later, they fall back down again as raindrops.

Drip, drop

Living Here

Animals and plants live in every part of the rainforest, from the tree tops to bushes on the ground.

Staying alive

The rainforest gives animals and plants food, water, and a place to live. Without these things, animals and plants die.

Monkeys live in rainforests.

Big and smelly

Make sure you don't get too close to the raffelesia plant. It is the biggest plant in the world – and it stinks of rotten meat. Disgusting!

Pooh!

Frog Forest

Frogs are everywhere in the rainforest. They jump around the forest floor, and climb up trees.

Dark and bright

Some frogs are dark to help them hide in the trees. Others are very colourful. The frog's bright colours warn others that it is **poisonous**.

Hands off!

Poisonous skin

Don't touch!

Poison dart frogs are **deadly**. There is enough poison in their skin to kill a big animal, such as a **jaguar**.

This tree frog uses sticky pads on its feet to climb up trees.

Bird World

Lots and lots of different birds live in rainforests. They make the rainforest colourful and noisy!

Nut cracker

The toucan likes to eat fruit and nuts. When it eats fruit, the **seeds** drop to the ground and grow into new trees.

Bee hummingbirds fly among rainforest trees.

Keep flapping

Super small

The bee hummingbird is so small it can sit on the tip of a pencil. It flaps its tiny wings up to 200 times a second.

Creepy Crawlies!

From beautiful butterflies to huge spiders, rainforests are full of creepy crawlies and insects.

Cleaning up

Dead animals and plants lie on the rainforest ground. They are eaten by beetles and **cockroaches**.

Beautiful

Killer bug

The assassin bug is small but deadly. It jumps on passing insects then sucks out their insides. Horrible!

Cockroaches eat any dead animals lying around.

15

Staying Alive

It's not easy for animals in the rainforest. But they have amazing ways of staying alive.

Sssss

If the king cobra snake is frightened, it will attack. It rises up until it is as tall as a human man – then bites!

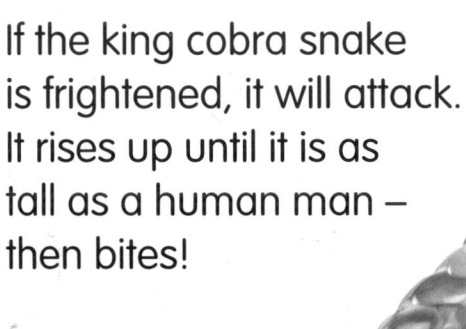

One bite from a king cobra can be deadly.

Vampires

Vampire bats drink blood to stay alive. They even drink human blood! They bite their prey, then lick its blood.

Slurp, slurp

Special Plants

Some of the things we use every day are made from rainforest plants.

Chocolate forest

Soap, bubble gum, and chocolate are just some of the things made from plants that grow in the rainforest.

We need rainforests

Keeping well

People who live in rainforests make medicines from rainforest plants. Many of our medicines are made from these plants, too.

Rainforest people know which plants are safe to use as medicines.

In Danger

Half of the world's animals and plants live in rainforests. But people are chopping down rainforest trees for wood and to build on the land.

Lost forever

Every second, an area of rainforest the size of a football pitch is chopped down.

Orangutans and other animals will die out if their rainforest trees are cut down.

You can help

Help to save the rainforests by:
* Telling people about the dangers to rainforests.
* Raising money for a **charity** that helps rainforests.

Save our trees

Glossary

charity group of people who try to help people, animals, or places that are in danger

cockroaches beetles that feed on rubbish and rotting food

deadly can kill

jaguar big cat that lives in rainforests

pitcher plant plant that has a jug-like part into which animals fall or crawl. Once the animal is inside, the plant eats it.

poisonous makes you very ill or kills you if it gets inside your body

seeds small parts of plants that can grow into a new plant